PREPARING FOR ADOLESCENCE
Answers
for Parents

James B. Stenson

D1173591

Scepter Publishers
Princeton, NJ

Nihil obstat: Joseph Penna, JCD
         Censor Librorum
Imprimatur: Patrick Sheridan
         Vicar General
         Archdiocese of New York
                              March 1, 1990

Books by James B. Stenson:

- *Upbringing: A Discussion Handbook for Parents of Young Children*

- *Lifeline: The Religious Upbringing of Your Children*

- *Preparing for Adolescence: Answers for Parents*

- *Preparing for Peer Pressure: A Guide for Parents of Young Children*

- *Successful Fathers*

- *Anchor: God's Promise of Hope to Parents*

Available from Scepter Publishers
(800) 322-8773 or www.scepterpublishers.org

Preparing for Adolescence was originally published as Scepter Booklet No. 185-186.

© 1989 Scepter Publishers

This edition © 2001 Scepter Publishers

Printed in the United States of America

ISBN 1-889334-35-9

Contents

Introduction:
Long-Term Planning

This book is principally for parents of young children, people whose youngsters are still several years away from high school. It outlines the characteristics of adolescence, and it studies the most troublesome questions that today's teenagers pose to challenge their parents' values.

This approach to adolescent issues—a preview of coming distractions, as it were—naturally gives rise to some questions. Why discuss adolescents' problems with parents of young children? Why and how should younger parents take interest in these issues now, when they're already busy trying to raise a young family? The general answer to these questions is: Because it's necessary.

For parents, the passage of their children through adolescence can be either wretched or richly rewarding depending (among other things) on the parents' clear-headed preparation for it. If young parents think deeply about adolescent issues now, years ahead of time, they can avoid serious problems later. In fact, the years when their children are in high school can be one of the most interesting and satisfying periods of their family's life.

Why do I say this? Let me explain.

First, long-term planning is intrinsically necessary to successful parenthood—yet it's frequently neglected. Many parents, perhaps most, are so wrapped up in the day-to-day and week-to-week tasks of family life that they seldom think seriously about the end result of all their effort: namely, what kind of character their children will have when they are grown men and women. Will they be mature, confident, responsible adults who live by Christian principles? Will their marriages be stable, happy, and permanent? (If present statistics hold true, about half of today's youngsters will be divorced by age 30.) Will the children make it through the challenges of adolescence with their faith and character and values intact—or will they be thrown off track? These and similar questions can form a basis for deep reflection and action now so that the children can grow up well.

Secondly, a great many parents are thrown back when their children reach adolescence because they are unprepared for it. All teenagers are more-or-less rebellious. As part of their natural longing for independence, adolescents challenge the values and authority of their parents. They want to know why certain moral values oblige them. They need to know why the line between right and wrong is drawn where it is. The simple reply they heard in childhood—"Because we say so..."—is no longer adequate for them. They need reasons. They need confident and reasonable explanations.

This is where so many parents are at a loss. Parents who have not thought deeply about moral issues, or at least not for a long time, are uncertain how to answer their adolescents' questions. Since they lack informed convictions, they are wavering in authority, inconsistent in their positions, and edgily defensive. Relations between parents and teens can thus deteriorate into emotional standoffs, shouting matches, power struggles, and the parents' growing sense of helplessness in the face of defiance.

It's important for parents to realize that their children need clear moral direction in adolescence. Most of young people's challenges are really strategic probes to test their parents' values. Deep down, most children want to grow up and do the right thing; but they need clear, confident explanations of what the right thing really is. Being highly uncertain of themselves, they're highly critical of everything and everyone around them. Though they'd be loath to admit it, they earnestly—sometimes desperately—need and want decisive moral leadership. That's where this book comes in. If parents can get a preview of what challenges lie ahead, they can prepare realistically for the future. In these pages we have outlined some of the most common questions that teenagers raise with their parents. After each, we've provided some reasoned and reasonable answers. All of these, we must emphasize, have come from experienced parents—men and women who have found these explanations effective in dealing with their teenage children.

The answers here are by no means comprehensive and exhaustive. Our hope is that young parents will take the time to think the questions and answers through, talk them over extensively, and—very importantly—discuss them with older, more experienced parents as well as with couples their own age. Discussing these issues with friends, with people whose judgment is trustworthy, should provide much practical advice and useful approaches for dealing with the children later, when the time comes.

This sort of long-range preparation has helped many parents whom we know. Fathers and mothers who have thought about these issues and discussed them with others have found several significant advantages.

For one thing, their own confidence is boosted enormously. Far from over-worrying about their children's future in high school, they look forward to giving final form to their children's character and conscience during one of the most interesting periods of life. Holding the hope that their kids will be adultlike rather than childlike in adolescence, they start to take steps now to bring this about. In other words, thinking positively about the children's adolescence affects the way they form the youngsters while they're small. There's a more continuous and steady direction to the children's upbringing, with adolescence thus becoming the final and most formative stage, even the most interesting and enjoyable.

Another effect is the way they can deal with the children later. When the children are looking for guidance in adolescence, the parents are ready. They have clear, reasonable answers that they themselves thoroughly understand and believe. The parents' moral leadership can therefore be calm, articulate, balanced (fair), and confident. There's no need for emotionalism or defensiveness. On the contrary, the young people can look to their parents with confidence. Their parents' level-headed teaching can form the basis for their own moral lives as adults-in-the-making. The inner strength of the parents' conscience, and the children's resultant respect for it, can strengthen the children's resistance to the allurements of materialism and peer pressure. This has worked. Parents have done this successfully.

Finally, there is the advantage of parental peer support. When parents meet with other couples to discuss their children's common future, they often become deep friends. They offer each other experienced advice and encouragement; they suggest different approaches and give objectivity to potentially emotional situations. They stand ready to help each other later, when their children grow into adolescence together.

Parents today need this sort of outside support from close friends. For generations, parents could rely on family members and close neighbors to give encouragement, sympathy, and advice. They could help with objectivity and sometimes humor. Parents today, isolated as they normally are, need to go out of their way to form this supportive network. After all, when the children are in high school, the teens have daily contact with dozens of energetic peers, whose rebelliousness and solidarity lend confidence, if not aggressiveness, to the adolescents' defiance at home. Parents therefore need a counteractive peer support of their own. This means relying on friends who share common values and common hope for the children's future.

There seems to be, as an inexorable fact of life, a sort of balance in raising children. You either pay now or you pay later, but either way you pay. Parents who put little trouble into raising their children as youngsters wind up paying dearly later, when the kids are grown. But those who put thought and conscientious effort into the kids' youngest years manage to find enjoyment and satisfaction later. The work put into the children's youth and adolescence pays great dividends. Over time, the children grow to become responsible, confident men and women who live by Christian principles—and they can grow to be like this before they're out of their teens.

Other parents have done this. So can you.

Reflections on Adolescence

What follows here are some general observations about adolescence. All of them, for whatever they're worth, derive from my twenty years' experience in secondary education. During this time I have known hundreds of families from all walks of life, and I've seen many young people grow from infancy to young parenthood. My study of this subject has been helped by the intelligent observations of many professionals who work with youth—teachers, coaches, psychologists, spiritual directors. Most valuable of all, however, has been the experience shared with me by conscientious, successful parents—people who have enjoyed seeing their children grow up well.

The generalizations below are by no means a comprehensive, exhaustive treatment of adolescent psychology and related family issues. I've simply tried to provide food for thought, some matters for reflection and discussion. If you, as parents of youngsters, want a fuller picture of these issues, then find some experienced parents to discuss them with. These people are the real experts. Their own stories of successes and mistakes are the most valuable guidance you can receive.

In other words, I have tried here to provide a framework for young parents to bring their thinking into clear, specific focus—so that they can discuss the issues between themselves and then approach other, more experienced parents with clear, specific questions.

Let's begin this discussion then with a note of hopeful, cautious optimism.

There's a prevailing myth in our society, much trumpeted in countless "parenting" books, that adolescence is a traumatic, agonizing, emotionally overwrought experience for parents and teens alike. This is not necessarily, or even typically, true. In my opinion, much of this myth derives from the negative personal experience of many parenting-book authors and the people with whom they associate; their own philosophical permissiveness has had detrimental effects on the children they know, and they've generalized about this dysfunctional experience.

Successful Parents

It seems to be a fact that most families throughout Western history, and most families outside our Western culture today, have had little serious trouble raising their children through adolescence. The solidity of the family seems to be critical to this success. But even today in Western societies, where the family's solidarity has taken a beating, countless parents do a fine job in raising their children well.

My colleagues and I have known many such parents over the years. Let me sketch a composite picture of their characteristics here:

• Successful parents maintain a clear ideal, a well-focused concept, of what kind of adults they want their children to become: competent, responsible, generous men and women who live confidently by Christian principles. They think of their children's future character, and not too much about their future careers.

• With this vision before them, they maintain a steady and consistent teaching of responsibility all the way from infancy through adolescence. Their discipline through the high-school years is a continuation and refined development of everything they taught before. They shift gears, as it were, and pick up speed, but they remain essentially on track.

• Invariably they are people who have clear moral convictions, and they live by them. When they have to lecture their teens from time to time (as all parents do), they are simply verbalizing what the children can see for themselves in the way the parents live. In other words, there's a consistency between their principles and their actions; they teach mostly by example.

• The father takes a more prominent role in guiding the children as they move through adolescence.

He works as a partner with his wife; he does not relegate "kids' things" to her. If anything, he exercises more influence than he did when the children were younger.

• They are aware of the many moral dangers to their children's welfare—to their earthly and eternal happiness—but they are not overly protective of the children nor hostile to society. They want their children to be strong, not "protected"—strong enough in conscience and character to handle these challenges themselves. Long-range, they want their children to form (or re-form) their culture, not merely to react to it. They look forward to their children's growing up, becoming young men and women before they're out of their teens.

• In guiding their children's lives, they do not permit what they disapprove of. They're confident enough to withstand the children's emotional resistance and clash of wills. They sense, quite rightly, that the children must have practice in denial if they're ever to develop a power of self-denial. They know that the kids need help, in the midst of emotional entanglements, to learn where the line is drawn between right and wrong. Sometimes parents need to show the line forcefully by putting their foot down.

• They maintain constant communication with their children, as they have always done since the kids were toddlers. They understand their children well and, just as importantly, the children understand them. The kids know all about their parents' personal history, their judgment and convictions, their mistakes and successes, their hopeful expectations for the family. The children know that the parents have confidence in their integrity and character—because they have confidence in themselves and confidence in God's loving providence.

• Frequently, these successful parents have several close friends who provide encouragement and support for their parental efforts. Consequently they do not feel isolated. In any case, they have strong religious convictions to rely upon. Quite often, they have a spiritual director, someone who helps them put prayer at the center of family life. The children's lives are, after all, entirely in God's hands. The parents see themselves carrying out his will for the young lives whom he has entrusted to their care.

This picture is, as we've said, just a sketch of the essentials. Individual parents vary considerably—in temperament, family history, outlook, family rules, approaches to disciplined guidance, and the like. Regardless of these differences, however, successful parents seem to all have four fundamental elements in common: (1) a clear vision of their children's future; (2) a determined will to make this ideal become a reality; (3) a commitment to their children's future happiness (especially in their future marriage); and (4) a reliance on God's help in living up to this commitment's implicit responsibilities.

We have to be realistic. Even successful parents experience problems, setbacks, disappointments along the way. Responsibility always calls upon us to surpass ourselves, and this means persistent work. But it's worth it. By and large, all things considered, responsible and conscientious parents manage to emerge victorious. They and their children are winners.

With these general considerations in mind, let's turn to look at some typical features of adolescents, along with some insights and bits of advice provided by experienced parents. These form a useful background for considering the questions and answers in the next section of this study.

Features of Adolescents

1. Adolescents have a strong tendency to assert independence from their parents. This is a normal, natural, and even necessary part of their growing up. Sooner or later, after all, they must become independent; the years between 12 and 17 are a preparation for this big step.

Anytime a sharp tension arises in human relationships, it is generally because a truth is being either denied or ignored. In modern Western society, tensions between parents and teenagers arise from an imbalance between freedom (independence) and responsibility. Though the teens' minds and bodies are essentially those of young adults, our society keeps adolescents in a state of childlike dependence at home. The teens have new access to adult-level powers—power to beget children, to spend substantial sums of money, to come and go as they please (usually with more physical freedom than their parents enjoy), to spend abundant leisure time in unsupervised activities, to obtain and use alcohol and other controlled substances. Though they possess these adult powers, they normally lack the concomitant responsibilities that fall upon full-grown adults. The central truth of moral life—that freedom must be counterweighted by responsibility—is thrown off-balance. Hence the tensions between parents and their teenage children.

For this reason, parents' formative efforts with their adolescents must emphasize assumption of responsibility. Parents have to work at this, and it isn't easy. But it isn't impossible either. At base, most teens really want to grow up, but they need to learn what this means. Life isn't play. Amusement doesn't bring really deep happiness. Real victory in adult life comes from the responsible, conscience-grounded exercise of our freedom. Other people need our strengths in the business of living. Teens who accept responsibility grow up quickly; those who don't can remain adolescent-like even into their 20's, or later. Ask any marriage counselor or specialist in drug rehabilitation.

2. Someone once said that living with a teenager is like sharing your home with someone suffering from a mild case of temporary insanity. This isn't altogether inaccurate.

The hormones coursing through an adolescent's growing body are powerful chemical reagents. Like many other biochemical substances, they sometimes have psychoactive side effects, leading to wide mood swings (giddy elation to sullenness and back again) and outbursts of semi-irrational behavior. Thirteen-year-olds withdraw into themselves for no apparent reason. Fifteen-year-olds enjoy arguing for its own sake, probing mercilessly for flaws in logic. Teens exaggerate faults in themselves and others. All in all, their behavior is often unpredictable and slightly nutty.

The key thing to remember is this: Don't take it personally. This is difficult because they seem "rational," and we adults quite naturally react to incivility and rudeness with annoyance or anger. But it is important to cultivate a certain detached view of things (without seeming unconcerned about the children) and to remain as calm and steadfast as possible, riding out the provocations with patience and equanimity. Shouting matches resolve nothing. The teen's own uncontrolled emotionalism (which is, as we've said, not entirely his fault) positively needs your confident control of things. Sometimes it helps a lot to remember what you went through at 15. (If

you don't remember, or even if you think you do—
ask your own parents.)

In any event, try to have the same love and de-
tachment from annoying provocations that you would
have, say, with a cranky, absent-minded elderly loved
one. The brain-chemistry situations are rather similar. Sooner or later, the body chemicals will settle
down into normal balance, as they did with you, and
you'll have wholly rational relations with your children once again. In the meantime, they need your
firm direction and loving understanding to lead them
through the valley of shadows.

3. The dominant mind-set of adolescents is uncertainty, though this is often manifested in stubbornness and resentment regarding rules or limits.
Consequently they need signs of certainty from you
and other responsible adults.

They need your assuredness and certainty of purpose. This is where many parents fail. Lacking clearly
articulable convictions, many parents are unsure how
to deal with their children's challenges. These people
try to compensate by exercising control for its own
sake, or they retreat into permissiveness, letting their
uncertainty override their misgivings. They thus fail
to provide external direction to kids who have no
internal direction of their own. The teens can thus
go out of control altogether, and this can be devas-
tating, even tragic.

The kids also need your confidence in them. They
have to see that you are proud of their inner strengths
and are certain that these will develop soon into full
maturity. It helps a lot here, as when the children are
small, to give them specific praise where they deserve it. Most parents tend to give only general praise
but highly specific correction. The children need

concrete specificity in both areas, commendation as well as constructive criticism.

Related to this, they need to pull out of themselves. Teens are acutely conscious of their appearance; they spend hours looking at themselves in the mirror, and they're not sure they like what they see. People who spend time preoccupied with themselves (adults as well as teens) become melancholy, almost depressed; they exaggerate problems and ignore the needs of people around them. For this reason, teens need to feel needed. It enhances their self-worth and develops maturity of judgment. Significant help around the house, volunteer work in hospitals and nursing homes, tutoring the disadvantaged, helping the poor—all of these give depth to young people's character, showing them how to use their new-found powers to give strength and consolation to others. The teens thus also come to learn that generous service brings deeper satisfaction than any number of amusements.

4. In many families with several children, parents are frequently tempted to treat all children as if they were about the same age, or rather as if they were variations around an average age. The oldest children thus often complain that they are treated too much like the younger ones. There's some merit in this complaint. Since the oldest children are older, and since they bear more responsibility in the family, they should have more freedom, within reason. They could and should have a later bedtime, for example, and more time with friends and a greater degree of privacy. If they really act responsibly at home, they deserve correspondingly greater freedom. The freedom-duty balance works both ways. It's only fair.

5. Young people who have been raised well since childhood generally respond well to appeals for fair-

ness. Of all the virtues, the sense of justice (which kids call "fairness") is the one that develops earliest and most deeply. It's a sound basis for making correction where necessary, even more effective than appeals to authority: "It's not fair to your mother to make her worry by staying out late without telephoning." Or: "It's not fair to embarrass our family in public with your dress and inconsiderate manners. We know you have enough good judgment to recognize this."

6. Many parents make a sound distinction between two kinds of lying: Some lies are told impulsively out of self-defense. (Lying is, after all, the only real defense children have against adult power.) The other lying, much more serious, is the coldly deliberate falsehood; it attempts to cover up cowardice or serious wrongdoing, and it is dishonorable.

It's unrealistic to presume that teens, especially young teens, will never lie. Some parents handle the problem this way: When they suspect that their child is lying, they say, "I'll give you a half-hour to think this over in your room. At that time, I want you to tell the full truth of the matter on your honor. Whatever you say, I will accept as the truth. But remember, our trust in your word, in your very integrity, is at stake. If you admit that you blurted out a lie before, you will be punished, of course. But we will know that your word of honor can be trusted. Nothing is worth losing our trust in your integrity. It's one thing to lie through a lapse in judgment; it's another thing to be a liar. So think it over...."

Naturally, parents can use this tactic most effectively with teens if they've used it since the children were small. A family custom like this is immensely valuable.

By the way, one of the most corrosive and destructive effects of teenage drug use is that it turns kids into liars. Teens with troubles in this area will go to any lengths to hide their wrongdoing. This is another reason why parents must cultivate, from youngest childhood, the children's sense of personal honor. The truth must always come first.

7. Around the ages of 15 and 16, young people need serious reading. It's remarkable to see how quickly their minds grow in powers of abstraction and sensitivity around 16. They are ready and able to study serious social issues and questions of morality in depth. They need, therefore, to read newspapers, news magazines, biographies, history, great literature. They're often surprised at how much they understand and like this sort of reading, especially since it may have seemed pointless and boring even a couple of years before.

Two practices help a lot here. First, TV-watching should be kept to a minimum. That is, programs should be selected beforehand and thus watched with some critical discernment. Secondly, parents can encourage conversation about social issues and current events around the dinner table and at other times. The older children especially will take to this. Keep in mind, however, that teens like argument for its own sake. Some discussions may, therefore, turn into lively debates. There's nothing wrong with this, and it can even be healthy. Besides, occasionally the kids might be right.

In this area, too, a long-standing practice in the family (i.e., minimal TV and extensive dinner-table discussion) can have its greatest effect when the kids are teens. Start it when the kids are young and you'll reap the fruits later. Other parents have found this again and again.

One final related matter in this area: The publishing industry has turned out literally tons of pulp-books for subteen girls, many of them highly touted for being "realistic," "appealing to the real-life situations" of 12-year-old females. These books portray supposedly typical junior-high-school girls in true-life situations, mixing in sentimental moralizing with frank discussion of amoral sexual behavior. In effect, they're soap operas for subteens.

Aside from the soft-prurient content of such books, they are at best a waste of time. This is narcissistic literature. Girls this age need to get out of themselves and read about real people in the world at large. They need a window on life, not a mirror. (Experienced, savvy parents check out the moral content of books published for sub-teens over the last 25 years.)

If parents know some experienced teachers who share their values (and they should go out of their way to do this), they can ask for personal recommendations in reading. The parents don't have to read along with their children; most don't have time anyway. But the kids can discuss their reading at dinnertime.

Before the invention of television, this was a custom in many families: one person would read a book, or sometimes read aloud for the family, and then everyone would comment. A lot of learning went on this way.

8. A useful gift for teens is a personal calendar/notebook. After age 15, they usually need one anyway. They should use this to mark appointments, note deadlines, set objectives on a timeline. Time management is, after all, another term for self-control. It's a big breakthrough for young people's maturity when they come to see that neglect, like bad mistakes, can have disastrous consequences. A calendar/notebook helps a lot to clarify this fact of life.

9. Another important distinction for teens to understand is the difference between popularity and respect. Adolescents ache to be liked, to be accepted favorably by their peers. Their emotions in this area often make them blind to the importance of earning people's respect, and of maintaining one's self-respect.

Therefore parents should go out of their way to teach some fundamental facts of interpersonal relations: Friendship is based on mutual respect, not on shared amusement. There's a difference between a sidekick—an accomplice in amusement—and a real friend. An apparent friendship without this respect is called familiarity, and it eventually breeds contempt. People may like us for the laughs we provide, but this doesn't mean they like us personally; it certainly doesn't mean they respect us. It isn't worth losing self-respect in order to be "popular"; sooner or later, people will drop us and move on to other amusements.

People of all ages, adults as well as peers, will respect us if we display strength of character. This sometimes takes effort, but it's worth it. People who respect us at first will eventually come to esteem us deeply, to love us for what we are. This is much more important than being "liked."

10. Discussions of sexual morality should deal, among other things, with preparation for marriage. Dating is not just a social activity. More deeply, it's a long-term preparation for a stable and happy married life. Having many friends of the opposite sex leads to understanding psychological and temperamental differences between men and women. It's interesting, even fascinating, to study the richness and variety of people's personalities. This learning leads over time to an intelligent framework for evalu-

ating people of both sexes, which, in turn, is crucial for courtship and the final choice of a spouse.

It's important for kids to realize that the teen years are meant for friendship, not for extended romance. Young people can fall in and out of love. In itself, this is harmless. But keeping constant, exclusive company with one attractive person can and does lead to serious problems. This isn't theory. It's fact.

Moreover, at some point boys and girls must be taught the importance of self-restraint and personal honor. Girls are normally unaware, for example, how immodesty in dress and intimacy of contact can inflame boys' passions. Unwittingly, just by seeking tender "romantic" situations, they can create serious moral problems for boys their age. Girls must be warned, therefore, about this explosive flash point in boys' emotional nature, an important temperamental difference between the sexes; one that can't be trifled with.

Boys, for their part, need appeals to their manly sense of honor. Since they're usually attracted to girls for their looks (a mistake, but they'll find this out later), they assume that girls are also swayed by Hollywood-style good looks. They need to know that girls tend to be more impressed by character. Girls look to a young man who is both considerate and tough-minded, kind and self-controlled: someone who will care for his future family and be strong enough to provide for it.

Boys in their later teens are receptive to discussion about their future lives as husbands and fathers. This sort of talk pulls them out of the dating-and-dancing social swirl, giving them serious consideration for the not-too-distant future. This sort of discussion, either as father-to-son or as mother-to-son, is an excellent way to discuss the moral issues of dating: considerateness, self-control, protectiveness, a sense of honor for one's date. As old-fashioned as it may seem, boys enjoy thinking of themselves in chivalrous terms—protecting and taking care of young women their age.

"Lady" and "gentleman." These are the concepts we're discussing here. The terms aren't used much in our time, perhaps because of the general decline of self-respect and habitual respect for others in our society, along with the erosion of self-restraint.

Thinking of your small children as future ladies and gentlemen is a helpful frame of reference for their upbringing. There really is a connection between habitual good manners in childhood ("please" and "thank you") and chastity in adolescence. Respectful, self-controlled behavior can't be taught overnight, when the kids turn 13.

11. One of the best advantages of preparing in advance for children's adolescence, especially by consulting with parent "veterans," is the ability to formulate reasonable and clear rules. Adolescents, like all of us, need to know what's expected of them. More to the point, they need to know ahead of time what consequences will follow from disobedience or thoughtless neglect. Thinking out these consequences as built-in parts of the rules is very helpful in dealing with teens. It cuts down on heated arguments. It eliminates misunderstandings (a common source of family friction) and reinforces the children's sense of responsibility.

Bear in mind that teens generally move in a social environment that fosters irresponsibility. They are free to exercise powers and make choices without much regard for consequences. Since society treats teens as large-sized children rather than young adults, someone else (parents, taxpayers) usually winds up paying for the teens' errors and neglect.

This stance is, of course, unrealistic. Adult life generally doesn't work this way. Grown-ups are free to make any number of choices, but they personally have to live with the results, for good or for ill. Adolescence is the time of life for making acquaintance with this reality.

Consequently, any set of rules must be accompanied by a clear explanation of what will follow if the rules are not complied with. The possibility of punishment thus appears as a fact, not a threat. If a teen then freely chooses to disobey a rule, he is also freely choosing to accept the promised consequence.

So, for example, if a teenage son stays out beyond his curfew, the parents can approach him the following day. (Late-night heated arguments are generally agonizing and ineffective all around; discussion of infractions should, wherever possible, wait until tempers have cooled.) The parents can approach their son and say: "You understood, didn't you, why we insisted that you return by 11:00 o'clock?... And you also understood that, if you came in later, you'd not go out again at night for a month?... Fine, then let's proceed as planned."

For certain, the teens will not like taking punishment; none of us like living with unpleasant consequences. But once emotions have settled, they have to admit that it's fair. Remember, a sense of fair play, of justice, is eminently important to teenagers. What causes them outrage is arbitrariness, inconsistency, and excessively harsh penalties imposed heatedly on the spur of the moment. Moreover, arguments about the consequent punishment draw attention away from the rule itself and the reasons for following it. The teens may not be out of line in resenting an unexpected and disproportionate punishment, and their anger would tend to cloud over the central lesson at issue.

No matter how you look at it, therefore, careful planning about ground rules is essential, not only for the children's growth in responsibility but also for family harmony. Here, as in so many other matters, the advice of experienced parents is invaluable.

12. There's no such thing as a perfect family or a perfectly behaved adolescent. Even in the best of families, some things can and occasionally do go wrong. All of us have memories of blunders we've made, mistakes that make us squirm with embarrassment to remember them. Keep this in mind when dealing with your teenagers.

Even a thoroughly well-formed young person can sometimes make a stupid mistake, almost always because of bad judgment, not out of bad will. The social pressures on teens these days are enormous, and sustained, flawless resistance is almost heroic. You can always hope for perfection in your children but don't expect it.

An occasional lapse, therefore, is not a cause for despair. If your son comes home from a party one night inebriated, or if your daughter tries a joint of marijuana, it's not the end of the world. You should, of course, take swift, decisive action to teach a firm lesson, but don't assume that your child is launched on the road to ruin. Sometimes kids can learn a lot from an isolated mistake.

In adolescence as in childhood, the kids need to see that you distinguish between their behavior and their very selves. You love them unconditionally, no matter what happens. You love them so much that you commit yourself to correcting their faults, and thereby build their character. You "hate the sin, but love the sinner," as the Scriptures enjoin us. You love them too much to let their faults become habitual.

For this reason, an expression of disappointment is much more effective than outrage: "We're disappointed that you let us down this time, but we're confident that you won't make the same mistake twice." This approach underscores your love for them personally, your high expectations for their growth in maturity. It shows that your discipline derives from your love.

13. Finally, it's important to start young. If you ask experienced parents (as I have) what they'd do differently if they had to raise their children through adolescence again, most would tell you, "We would have started earlier, when the kids were young."

Long before adolescence, children have to acquire the virtues that make for strong character: faith, hope, charity, prudence, justice, fortitude, temperance. (These last four "cardinal virtues" would today be called by different names: sound judgment, a sense of responsibility, persistent toughness, and self-control.) Children simply can't start acquiring responsible judgment and self-control beginning at age 13. The teenage years are a time for refined, mature development of these strengths, not their foundation from scratch.

Therefore: Do you want your children to "say no" to drugs later? Then don't indulge them now with junk food, big allowances, and impulse buying. Do you want them to treat the opposite sex with respect? Then insist now that they show respectful good manners to everyone, starting with parents and siblings. Do you want them to be responsible later? Then hold them accountable now—for homework, the appearance of their room, the timely fulfillment of their chores around the house. Do you want them eventually to have a stable, permanent marriage? Then teach them generosity, self-denial, and the importance of keeping commitments. And so on.

All moral development is a progression from childish selfishness to generous responsibility. The vices of childhood (self-willfulness and appetite gratification) are often overshadowed in the parents' vision by the children's cuteness. But, if unchecked during youth, these tendencies grow to be monstrous flaws in adolescence. Well-meaning, indulgent parents have awakened abruptly, shocked, to find their teenage children out of control. This happens literally every day.

You will find, as many parents have, that studying what to expect later leads inexorably to making changes now. Consider yourself blessed to be forewarned in time. We all have only one chance to raise children right. A great many parents would give anything to be in your position: to set matters straight from the very beginning, when the children are still open to be formed.

So, be thankful that you have this chance with your children. Be concerned about them but don't overworry. Fear is a poor basis for children's upbringing. Your teens and younger children need to see you confident and on top of life. They need to see in you a model of principled judgment and good humor in the face of life's challenges. With God's help, your own common sense, and the advice of good friends, you can pull this off successfully.

To your teenage children, then, may you be—as St. Peter urged the earliest Christians—"...ready always with an answer to everyone who asks a reason for the hope that is in you." (1 Peter 3:15)

Questions and Answers

What follows here is a compilation of the most common issues that arise between teenagers and their parents. For the sake of simplicity, we've put them in question-and-answer form. As you'll see, the questions are not always phrased the way teens would pose them; it's the issue we're dealing with, not its articulation. The answers are written as if spoken to the adolescents; but here too the form is simplified. The way the explanations appear here is more blunt and forthright than would normally (we hope) be the case in parent-teen conversation. In other words, the reader needs to take these ideas, think them over, discuss them with others, and then decide what would best fit family circumstances. Any such conversation with teens must come from well-reflected, sincere convictions. If your children are still small, you have time to form these thoroughly.

As any experienced parent can tell you, the cut and dried Q/A format here is by no means typical of the exchanges between parents and their adolescent children. The youngsters try to wheedle, argue, badger and otherwise work their way around firm parental explanations. Relentlessly, they look for flaws in reasoning and inconsistencies between principle and practice in the parents' lives.

This is why thinking these matters through now is so important. The more deeply set your principles are, the more readily you can defend and explain them. You leave the kids no "openings" to exploit. They thus come to see, and eventually to appreciate, why you've drawn the line clearly where you did—that all-important line between right and wrong that they need as near-adults, a set of standards to carry through life. Deep down, adolescents yearn for clear-cut, adult-level standards of how to live rightly. Your calm, level-headed direction in these matters—the result of your long-term preparation and sincere convictions—can thus lead your children steadily through the throes of growing up.

One final word: As you read the answers suggested here, you may find that you don't entirely agree with what is said. There's nothing wrong with this, but I would ask you to keep an open mind about it. All of what appears here, as said before, has come from the experience of other parents. If you discuss these matters with friends of your own, you may change your mind.

In any event, we hope the ideas outlined here will provide you with useful matters for reflection.

Q. *Why do you keep treating me like a child? Why don't you want me to grow up?*

A. It's understandable that you might think from time to time that you're being treated like a child. As parents, we sometimes have to correct you and give you clear direction; at other times, we have to restrict your freedom somewhat. But none of this means that we don't want you to grow up.

When we do have to give you clear direction, you should keep some important things in mind.

First, we are trying to build strengths in you. Because we love you, we want you to enter adult life with a strong character and conscience, our idea of true liberation. You have come a long way since childhood in developing your mind and will, and we're pleased with your progress. Because of your inexperience, you are capable of making mistakes, both in judgment and in action. A habit of mistakes is a weakness, and it is this that we're trying to correct. By learning from our experience, you can become stronger and more grown-up. This is what we're after.

Secondly, this desire for you to grow up soon—in responsibility as well as freedom—has been our ambition since you were a small child. Some parents, for reasons all their own, want their children to remain children for as long as possible. We have never thought this way. On the contrary, we have always seen you as an adult-in-the-making. As an adolescent, you are almost there. Our goal has been that you would have mature judgment and a sense of personal responsibility by the time you reached the later years of high school. Our present efforts to correct your residual remnants of childhood are, in our estimation, a fine-tuning of your growth in character.

Third, learning from other people's experiences and responsible judgment is a fact of adult life. It's by no means confined to relations between parents and small children. Almost all adults continually receive direction—sometimes as blunt commands—from bosses and other superiors. Everybody answers to somebody. What is called "obedience" in the family is called "co-operation" in adult society, but the principle is the same. Adults who want to progress in developing their powers go out of their way to seek experienced advice; they welcome direction from bosses, consultants, professionals, older people. To be sure, some people are inflexible about receiving direction; in doing so, they are often marked as immature and professionally stagnant. Such people get fired.

We understand that sometimes our correction bruises your feelings. It's frequently difficult for us adults to receive correction, too. But it's worth the trouble. Every time you say no to your feelings and your pride, you grow in powers of self-control. The experience of bending to directions from legitimate authority almost always makes us stronger one way or another. When you come to see the benefits of cooperation, and not just the discomfort, we'll know that you're arriving at real maturity.

How soon this happens is up to you. But we're confident it will happen eventually. Meanwhile we have to contend with the difficulties of giving direction, which you'll also learn about in time.

One last item: Be careful about ascribing motives to people. One of the hardest things in the world is to determine people's true motives. In fact, it's often tricky to determine our own motives in things, never mind someone else's. Ascribing ill motives to people is one of the greatest sources of injustice in the world. You owe it to people, as a matter of fairness, to presume good will on their part. We, your parents, have only one motive in our correction of your actions. That is our love for you—which means our steadfast commitment to your earthly and eternal happiness.

Q. *Why don't you trust me?*

A. It's very important to make a distinction here. We trust your integrity, but we must sometimes mistrust your judgment. You are assuming that a mistrust of your judgment means a lack of confidence in your honor. This isn't true.

We have full confidence in your earnest desire to do the right thing, to live according to a well-formed conscience. We know that we can trust your word of honor. Small children will, of course, lie on impulse if they're cornered; lying is their only real defense. But we know you have outgrown this weakness and that we can count on you, when you're put on your honor, to tell the truth and to try to do the right thing. You have character such that your intentions, your conscience, and your actions are all one. This is what is meant by integrity.

Your judgment is another matter. We have to face facts, and it's a fact that you lack experience in many areas of life. This is not your fault, and in fact it's not a moral fault at all. It's simply the truth of the matter, so you shouldn't take this assessment personally.

Having sound judgment is one of the signs of maturity. But sound judgment develops with time and with experience—vicarious experience at first and then personal experience. In short, one's judgment grows in strength through teaching and learning. Right now, you have to learn through our advice, our instruction, our own experienced judgment in certain matters. We sometimes have to say no to your wishes and feelings. Be patient. Over time (really just a few more years), we expect to see you grow in discernment about people and circumstances, and also in powers of self-control. The sooner we see your judgment approximating that of responsible adults, the sooner we can have confidence in your ability to handle yourself in difficult or potentially dangerous circumstances. At that point, you will have our trust entirely.

We understand that you may not like this position of ours, but we have to ask you to trust us. Once you've cooled down, and maybe grown up a bit, you'll see that it's reasonable.

After all, would you trust your little sister to play with your CD player, for example? Would you want her to plan the week's menu and buy the groceries for this house? There's no question that she has a good heart and wants to do the right thing. But you know that she lacks judgment in these areas simply because of her age and inexperience. Even if you did permit her to try her hand in these matters, it would have to be under close supervision. In any event, the handling of some responsibilities simply has to wait.

This process continues into adult life, too. Physicians work for years under supervision before they're certified to act on their own responsibility. Airline pilots undergo extensive education and training before they're licensed; and commercial pilots—even people with years of experience—receive periodic tests of their judgment in stress situations. No one is put in charge of a responsible position (that is, where he can cause damage to himself and others) until he has a proven record of sound judgment. This is a fact of life.

Q. *Why won't you give me freedom?*

A. The term freedom—like its counterpart terms authority, independence, rights, choice, options—is just another word for power. It's useful to consider the terms this way. Power to do what? Power for what purpose, or for whose benefit?

Nature has ordained it that freedom (power) must be directed by responsibility—that is, an ethical regard for how the use of that power affects the rights of others. This is why rights must be balanced by duties, and authority by checks and balances.

It's no exaggeration to say that most serious problems in the world today (the world you will soon enter as a full-grown adult) result from an imbalance between rights and duties, between freedom and responsibility. If someone has responsibility without a corresponding freedom, his life is miserable. If he has powers without responsibilities, he can do serious damage. Look around and see for yourself. There must be a balance.

Consider the powers that you have as a result of your age and today's social circumstances. Teenagers today have a lot of new powers suddenly within their grasp:

- power to beget children.
- power to obtain and abuse alcohol and other drugs.
- power to drive an automobile: almost a ton of steel, hard plastic, and glass.
- power to come and go as they please: more physical freedom than that enjoyed by adults.

In former times, most of these powers entered a young person's life just before real independence. Up until the 20th century, someone your age was considered a young adult in every sense of the term; people married or left home to begin their own lives before they were out of their teens. Consequently, the circumstances of marriage and professional life imposed serious responsibility just as young people came into the powers of adult life. There was a balance.

Today, however, most of your contemporaries in the Western world enjoy powers of adult life with almost none of the corresponding responsibilities. This literally irresponsible exercise of freedom has been exhilarating for young people but, in the long run, damaging for them and for our society. It has resulted in pregnancies, abortions, drunk-driving accidents, alcohol addiction, drug-related tragedies, vandalism, criminal records, and serious harm to families.

Our discipline—that is, our direction of your actions—is an attempt to help you learn to use your powers responsibly, to enable you to internalize an habitual sense of right and wrong. The word discipline doesn't mean "to punish." It's related to the word disciple and it really means "to follow." Many people your age follow their impulses, or their feelings, or their appetites and passions, or the latest fad of thought. What we're trying to do is give you something powerful to follow: a well-formed conscience.

Our discipline is for this alone: to make your conscience clear enough and strong enough to be a guide for your whole life.

Be patient. When you have grown and gone, you will answer to God, to your own family, and to society. In the meantime, you must answer to us, because we answer to God for your welfare and we love you too much to let you drift through life.

As you will see with your own children, no is also a loving word. Unless young people experience loving denial, they cannot form a healthy power of self-denial. And without this, they could find—as so many have—some part of their life completely out of control. An uncontrollable power means disaster, not freedom.

The most confident and deeply happy people you'll meet will be those who are on top of life because of their strong character and clean conscience and a purposeful direction to their life. On top of life—this is where we want you. With God's help, we're confident that you'll come to enjoy this self-mastery and thus be really free.

Q. *All the other kids my age can stay out later than I can. Why can't I stay out as late as they do?*

A. We don't know for a fact what curfew your friends' parents have set. In any event, this is beside the point. We don't answer for your friends or for their parents, but we do answer for you—to God, to our consciences, and even to the legal authorities. As long as we have these responsibilities, we must in justice have the corresponding level of authority.

We want to direct you to do the right thing and to know what the right thing is. We do not want to manage you. Because of your age, you have a certain freedom of movement. But, also because of your age, you have certain restrictions. What we are looking for is a reasonable meeting point between these two realities, which means a reasonable hour to return home.

Remember that it causes us, your parents, to worry a lot if you're not home by a reasonable hour. Given the many things that can go wrong among people your age, this is a perfectly understandable concern. Nobody has a right to cause serious anxiety to his loved ones without really sufficient reason. It's fundamentally unfair.

Time-management is another name for self-control. The better you are able to manage your time (by keeping an agreed-upon deadline), the more you give evidence of self-control. This, in turn, will lead to greater trust in your judgment and consequently a later stay-out hour. In other words, the sooner you demonstrate the adult traits of considerateness and reliability, the sooner you will enjoy our confidence in your maturity.

Since we're talking about adulthood, let's be realistic. Except for the idle rich, almost all adults return home from social occasions at a reasonable hour—only an hour or two later than the curfew we've set for you. After all, other people depend on their consciousness and energy the next day. This is true even on weekends. Though many teenagers today can and do live like the idle rich, we would hope you are not one of them. People of the leisure class throughout history have been more like children than adults. It is normal socially active adults whom you should emulate, and these people get in at a reasonable hour.

We also might add that adults generally call home if they expect to arrive later than a pre-arranged hour. This is done out of considerateness for our loved ones. Here, as in so many other things, we want you to think and behave like a responsible adult. Grown-ups care enough to call.

Q. *All the other kids my age enjoy wearing the latest designer clothes and having the latest electronic things. Why can't I? Why do you make me wait for things?*

A. Our direction in this area of shopping, of spending money, stems from two convictions of ours.

First, you are not just a "consumer," and we don't want you to think of yourself as one. You were not "born to shop." A large segment of our economy depends on people's impulse-buying as a result of vanity and insecurity and herd instinct. We want to give you practice in rising above these superficial motives. Many people who give themselves over to shopping for these reasons come to judge themselves and other people in terms of appearances. We want you to think more deeply than this.

Secondly, we see it as our responsibility to teach you, through a reasonable amount of practice, to exercise sound judgment and self-restraint in your personal affairs. This is why we insist that you wait a few weeks and think things over before you make a substantial purchase. If you do this, you'll find that you may not really need the item, or that you can get it elsewhere at a lower price, or that you can find a better and less expensive substitute. This is the way responsible adults use their financial resources.

After all, money is not just for "spending." There are plenty of young people in their 20's and even 30's who do think of it this way. In this, as in many other respects, such individuals retain the mental habits of young adolescence. Even though they work full-time, they still think of their jobs as sources of "spending money," and they live for the amusements and gadgets they can buy with it. Living as they do for comfort and leisure, they are a salesman's dream come true. Their preoccupation with pleasure leads them to be irresponsible and narcissistic, caring neither for children nor their own parents. A very great number of them wind up lonely and disappointed with life.

Money is a resource for the welfare of our loved ones and those in need. That's all it is. When it's used in this way, you find deep happiness.

This isn't just a quirky opinion of ours. It's the common experience of mankind. Every culture in history has witnessed how an excess of material riches weakens character and blinds people to earthly and eternal realities. Material scarcity, on the other hand, serves to strengthen character. It sharpens judgment, deepens a sense of responsibility, and gives us greater mastery over ourselves.

What we're looking for, really, is that you grow to be "poor in spirit." Our family, and indeed our whole society, has been blessed with material advantages. Compared with our ancestors or most people alive today on our planet, we live like wealthy aristocrats. Most people on earth have only one pair of shoes, if that. Most people struggle hard to get any food at all, and they are happy to get the same bland meal day after day. These people learn, through hard experience, the real sources of happiness in life: family solidarity, loyal friends, religious conviction, confidence in God's loving providence. Poverty, like any hardship, helps us set life's priorities in order.

A person's worth is measured by his character and his conscience—not his gadgets and possessions. As someone said: "Character is what you have left over if you happen to go broke."

Q. *Why can't I go steady like other kids my age? Do you want me to be unpopular?*

A. The custom of people your age "going steady" is really a leftover from the era when adolescents were considered to be near-adults, not just large-sized children. Formerly it was common for men and (especially) women to marry before the age of 20.

Within this framework, the normal stages of social development were: 1) awareness of the opposite sex; 2) mixed-group acquaintanceship; 3) personal friendship with several members of the opposite sex simultaneously; 4) extended (and largely exclusive) relationship with one in particular; 5) serious courtship and marriage. This was stretched out between the ages of 12 and 21.

Today, stages 1 to 3 take place in the last years of grammar school, while stage 4 remains a steady-state condition (with several people, one after another) until age 19 or early 20. It's ironic that these early stages should have been telescoped this way while the age for marrying has extended, on average, until age 26 or later.

It's also ironic that, for many young people, stages 3 and 4 are often reversed. Kids frequently "go steady" between the ages of 15 and 19, and then branch out to meet and know many friends.

There are sound practical reasons for you to hold off from "going steady" until you are older. Let's be realistic. Up until just a couple of years ago, you were scarcely aware of the existence of the opposite sex. You, like everyone else your age, have a lot to learn about the richness and diversity of personalities inherent in men and women. It is interesting and enjoyable to meet different types of people from the opposite gender, getting to know them as friends. The more friends you have, the more deeply you come to understand people, all kinds of people. This knowledge sharpens your judgment about people's character. You would find, among other things, that people often have qualities that don't appear clearly until you get to know them better. Appearances can be deceiving.

To look at it another way, it doesn't make much sense to suddenly become aware of half the people on this planet and then immediately confine yourself to knowing only one of them.

Aside from the question of judgmental development, there are also moral considerations.

Young people generally have more energy than judgment, and they frequently lack the life-experience necessary to keep emotional impulses under control. You shouldn't take this generalization personally; it's true of practically everyone. The emotional forces between young men and women are powerful. Under certain circumstances, they can get out of control. Male-female relationships have a built-in "escalator." Exclusivity and intimacy over time inevitably carry men and women to closer emotional bonds and an intensified urge for physical expressions of intimacy. If marriage is not a realistic possibility within the foreseeable future, getting on this "escalator" is an invitation to premature intimacy, personal frustration, and serious moral dilemmas. Our society is rife with teen pregnancies and the tragedy of abortion. Most of these, by far, happen among normal adolescents from perfectly normal family backgrounds.

We think it's reasonable to posit that such a situation is less likely to happen if boys and girls maintain a respectful distance from each other—that is, if they refrain from extensive time spent in each other's exclusive company. Powers of self-restraint and sound judgment generally (not always, but generally) increase with age. This is why society makes young people wait some years before driving an automobile or using alcoholic beverages. A great deal of experience has gone into this assessment. Similarly, you should wait until later before you keep steady company with someone of the opposite sex.

We repeat, this policy of ours is not intended to cut off your social development. On the contrary, we want you to meet and befriend many people in various social circumstances. We're confident that, with time, you'll come to see the reasons behind our position. In this, as in other matters, we are concerned for your long-range happiness.

As for the popularity issue, let's make one thing clear. We would be pleased if you are popular, but we would rather that you be respected. People can "like" each other for all sorts of reasons, some of them very superficial. People may "like" you simply because they find you amusing; shared amusement isn't the same thing as friendship. Real friendship is based on respect.

Respect, in turn, derives from people's perception of your strengths in character: your judgment, your sense of responsibility, your considerateness, your convictions, your self-control in the face of adversity. The more you work to develop your character, the more people will come to respect you, to hold you in high esteem, and to count you as a great friend. This is the only kind of "popularity" that matters in this world.

In any event, no matter what others think of you, the only really important thing is that you remain in the friendship of God. This is the basis for all significant human relations.

Q. *Why should I have to do chores around the house? Why should I have to clean up my room when I like it the way it is?*

A. Our home is a team operation, and your help is needed here to make for a livable and enjoyable environment. For years now, you have been on the receiving end of your parents' efforts to provide this sort of ambiance; simple justice demands that you repay this with some responsible work.

Since you have practically all the mental and physical powers of adulthood, it's fitting that you have some adult-level responsibilities as well. It's unreasonable for you to want it both ways: to enjoy the powers of adulthood while also enjoying the irresponsibility of small childhood. Among adults, only the idle rich live this way. If we consented to let you live like such people, we would be doing you—and your future spouse—a serious disservice.

One of the features of childhood is insensitivity to physical messiness. Seeing life exclusively as amusement, a small child scarcely notices the mess he makes of his immediate surroundings. Look, for example, at an infant eating in his high chair; he wears more food than he swallows.

No matter how you look at it, taking care of one's things and keeping up reasonable appearances are signs of mature responsibility and self-control.

So, too, is an awareness of other people's feelings. We, your parents, have feelings too—and, being adults, we are offended by the messiness of your room in an otherwise orderly house. When you come to "feel" the same way we do about slovenly disorder, we will have reason to judge that you're arriving at real, not make-believe, adulthood.

These are signs we look for when we must evaluate how responsibly you will handle the freedoms that you long for—a later curfew, dating privileges, part-time job, allowances, use of the car, and so on. Try to see it from our point of view: If you can't steer trash into your wastebasket, why should we think you can safely handle our car? If you can't manage affairs in your closet, why should we expect you to handle yourself at a late-night party? If you can't keep your feelings in check at home, how can we trust you to keep them under control elsewhere— especially where uncontrolled feelings can lead to trouble with drugs and alcohol?

We want to trust your judgment and self-control as soon as possible. The way you exercise control over your belongings will be one of our principal criteria.

Q. *Reading books is boring. Why should I read when there is so much else to do?*

A. Be careful about over-using the word "boring." Sometimes boredom comes from having one's powers unchallenged, underused. But it also can indicate a long-term habit of indulgence, a life centered around comfort of the body and idleness of the mind.

In other words, it is dull, boring people who complain most about boredom. Because they have so few self-initiated interests, they are themselves uninteresting. Habituated as they are to passive amusements, they don't know how to pursue new interests and thus become interesting people.

Throughout life, you will find people who enjoy thinking and learning. Such people are almost always interesting to know. They have lively dispositions and are often genuinely considerate people, warm friends. Even into old age, they seem to retain a certain youthfulness of spirit, an openness to new experiences and new ways of looking at things. The human spirit, when exercised frequently, seems never to grow old.

Reading worthwhile books is a way to meet the minds of interesting people, and to develop oneself to become this kind of person. Reading history and selective biographies is one way of learning about people of accomplishment: what problems they surmounted, what hardships they endured, what character and ideals made them extraordinary. Learning about such people is a great way to break out of the provincialism inherent in suburban living—where you associate almost exclusively with people just like yourself, in a physical environment that has no history.

Learning about the accomplishments of outstanding people serves to give depth and even wisdom to your judgment. It gives you an eye for the causes and implications of the events surrounding you. It gives you a sounder foundation for evaluating people, which is something vitally necessary in adult life. After all, mature judgment is largely experienced judgment. And we gain experience rapidly by study and reflective reading.

It's a fact that all the great leaders for the past several centuries had a lifetime habit of extensive reading. It's likely that their depth of judgment is what caused others to hold them in high esteem. We generally respect people who show a genuine respect for learning.

If you can read a page every two minutes, and you managed to read for even only a half-hour a day, you could read about eighteen books a year. With an hour a day, you could read almost forty.

But which books? The best way to find worthwhile books is to ask for recommendations from people whose judgment you respect. If you approach such people, you'll find that they read a lot.

The strengthening of your mind is so important that you simply must make time for it, just as you make time for exercise and for conversation with your friends. In all these cases, you are making a good investment of your time; time is, after all, a non-retrievable resource.

One time-use that must be apportioned carefully is television. Some programs on TV are beneficial for you, one way or another. They can teach you something, as with documentaries or comprehensive news analyses. They can introduce you to fine art, as with concerts or dramatic productions. Or they can draw you closer to family and friends, as when you watch sports together. This sort of television-watching is a sound investment of time.

What is not a sound investment is to watch, habitually and indiscriminately, programs of fluffy entertainment. These things are essentially live-action cartoons, dramatized comic books. They are to the mind what bubble gum is to the body—a pleasant but useless exercise. Nobody can live on bubble gum.

You're old enough to examine yourself honestly in this area. After you've watched several hours of bubble-gum programs, ask yourself some questions: How much do I remember of what I've just seen? What have I learned that I didn't know before? How else could I have used these past several hours? How am I better off—in any way whatsoever—for the time I expended in front of the tube?

One last thing, very important: As you grow older, your mind naturally grows in powers of understanding. This is especially true between the ages of 15 and 17. As you learn more about people and about life, you can acquire insight that you lacked even a couple of years before. Consequently, you may find that serious literature and history appeal to you much more than they did previously. A book that bores you at 14 may interest you at 16 and fascinate you at 18. Countless other people have had this experience. Will you? You won't know unless you try.

Q. *Why do you put restrictions on what I wear and the kind of music I listen to? When you were my age, didn't you adopt teen fashions in dress and music yourselves?*

A. In this issue, as with others, we are looking for reasonability. What's reasonable, not just for your likes and dislikes but for your long-term interests and our parental responsibilities?

It's reasonable that you would want to dress fashionably among your peers. A certain amount of social conformity is normal and even desirable. There's no intrinsic harm in adopting—up to a point—the styles in dress and music that manufacturers have concocted for you.

Let's not forget, while we're on the point, that teen fashions originate among certain profit-minded adults, not among teens themselves. This is a fact, and you should be aware of it. Adolescents who think that their own peers come up with these fashions are naive and unsophisticated; such youngsters are a salesman's dream. Most young consumers, it would seem, are unreflective followers. Teenagers, loaded down with spending money and eager for flashy novelty, are consumers par excellence.

You'll find as you grow older that teenage fashions change even faster than you do. For the sake of maximum profit, they have to. What you find "cool" and enormously attractive today will, in 25 years time, cause your children to scream laughing. Take it from us, the photos we take of you now will look hilariously funny to your children.

But let's get back to the present. What would cause us to draw the line with respect to your dress and choice of music? Let's clarify what will cause us to make restrictions in these areas:

1. If we see evidence that you are coming to judge people on the basis of fashion.

2. If you are patronizing music whose lyrics are offensive to our moral principles. Sexually-oriented lyrics are materialistic in outlook; they imply that people are merely things and may be treated like things. This we won't tolerate. We are obligated, as long as we are responsible for you, to register our disapproval of this outlook on life.

3. If your dress and interests in the pop culture show that you're taking it too seriously. Even the morally harmless aspects of this culture can cause damage to some impressionable young people. The culture is, after all, a deliberately contrived theatrical illusion. It's an entertainment make-believe, not a way of life. If you, like many other young people, start to confuse the two, we have to take steps to restore you to reality. You can enjoy this theatricalism up to a point, but don't believe it.

4. If the dress and appearance cause embarrassment to us as a family. Like it or not, people associate the extremes of pop-culture dress with the more sordid aspects of the culture: drug abuse, sexual permissiveness, unrestrained pursuit of pleasure, nihilism. Inasmuch as this judgment is untrue of your character, it is misleading and unjust, not just to you but to us as a family. Your own reputation and the honor of our family are extremely important, much more important than your fashion preferences.

5. If it absorbs too great a share of your funds.

The "generation-gap" argument may seem plausible on the surface, but it contains a serious flaw.

You can't adequately compare two things that are essentially different. It's true that there was a teen-culture a generation ago, in our time, with its distinctive fashions and music, similar to today. We say "similar" because the content and moral implications have changed drastically. A generation ago, drug abuse among normal teenagers was virtually unheard of. There was sexual promiscuity (as there always has been in every age), but society strongly disapproved of it; unlike today, people knew it was wrong. Abortion mills weren't advertised in the Yellow Pages. Any way you look at it, the moral climate has changed dramatically over the past generation.

If popular music in our day had contained sexually oriented lyrics, our parents would have forbidden us to patronize it. And they would have been right. Our teen music may have clashed with our parents' taste, but it didn't offend their principles. That's the difference.

The line, then, is between taste and morals. Morality is not merely a matter of social convention. It derives from man's nature and man's relationship with God. Consequently, we will permit (up to a point) whatever aspects of teen fashion and music are strictly matters of style. However, we will not permit what offends our moral convictions. Since both style and moral substance are intertwined today in a complicated way, we have to practice discernment. We shall have to require your cooperation in this regard as well as your trust in our responsible judgment.

When you later have children of your own, you will certainly have to exercise this discernment yourself. This you can do more effectively if you clearly remember the experience. So please bear with us. Right now, the moral climate shows no signs of turning upward in your lifetime. Your children's future happiness may depend on what you learn now about standing up for one's convictions. Though you presently may not like this arrangement, we're confident you will later come to see its rightness. Trust us.

Q. *Why do you always correct me about my manners? Why should I show respect to people I don't know? Especially to older people?*

A. It's been said that young people go through three stages in growing up:

- Child: "What can you do for me?"
- Adolescent: "Let me do this by myself!"
- Adult: "What can I do for you?"

All of moral progress consists of moving from concern for self to concern for others, starting with God. The immature (that is, the irresponsible) are self-preoccupied; mature people are preoccupied with others. As you'll learn with your own children, infants have to be taught to say "thank you." Then later to mean "thank you." They are then led to have an active awareness for the needs and rights and feelings of others.

We are pulled out of ourselves by our awareness of other people's necessities. Absolutely everyone has a right to be treated with regard for their intrinsic dignity. It is a mark of your maturity that you show your respect for this dignity by living courteously, starting with basics like "please" and "thank you."

People your age who are thoughtlessly discourteous have not moved from stage one of moral development; they are childishly self-centered. It is probably not entirely their fault, for courtesy has to be learned principally at home, from one's parents. Consistently inconsiderate teenagers have been missing this formation since infancy. We, as your parents, can't and won't let this happen to you.

One of the signs of greatness in an adult is how he or she treats strangers. (It is also the sign of a civilized people, a great nation.) As Our Lord taught us, everyone is our neighbor. He himself died for absolutely everyone, including his sworn enemies.

Even as a practical matter, it's in your interest to show courtesy to adults. Remember, it's more important to be respected than to be liked, but respect generally has to be earned. Adults are usually disposed to like young people, especially children. But they immediately form respect for a young person who shows them courtesy. In the eyes of adults, a well-mannered child or adolescent is, in all likelihood, self-disciplined and responsible. They assume that the young person is more like an adult than a small child.

As for the elderly, they especially deserve our affection and respect. As you look around, you will see the fruits of our civilization, a social structure that you will soon inherit as an adult. It was the elderly who planned, built, sacrificed and paid for the material advantages that we all now enjoy.

The oldest among them suffered through the worst economic disaster and the greatest military catastrophe in history. They emerged with their faith and values intact. These they have passed on to us as the fruits of their sacrifices and steadfast optimism. Their life was both hard and adventurous. You could enjoy hearing their stories, learning how they managed to triumph in life. They have a lot to teach you about character. All of us owe them our deepest gratitude and honor.

Q. *Your moral values are old-fashioned. Why shouldn't I be free to adopt the "new morality" of my own generation?*

A. If you knew much about history, you'd know that there's nothing new about the "new morality."

Outside of the Judaeo-Christian ethic, and before the Christian era, people have always lived pretty much the way that is currently glorified in the "new morality." They pursued unrestricted pleasure as an end in itself. They treated other people as if they were mere things. (This is the essential evil of materialism—seeing man as a thing.) They gave free rein to their passions and appetites, and they lusted after power.

The Roman civilization was similar to our own. At its best, it was efficient, economically productive, characterized by a strong and reasonably fair legal system. At its worst, it had the same vices with which we're so familiar: marital instability, abortion, gross social inequities, racism, pornography, sexual promiscuity, organized violence, genocide. The paganism of that era wasn't a religion so much as it was a way of life; it was essentially a hedonism hedged by superstition.

Then as now, many people were revolted by these materialistic excesses. Christianity spread rapidly in the Roman Empire because it was a light, a beacon of hope, to the many decent people surrounded by moral degeneracy. As our Faith triumphed, it brought a transformation in the social fabric. The Christian ethic brought with it a host of institutions for the betterment of man. Universities, orphanages, hospitals, schools for the poor, organizations to care for the destitute—all of these were promoted for centuries by Christians who took their faith seriously.

Naturally, throughout the Christian era, there have been people who've repudiated the Christian ethic and lived by the tenets of old-fashioned materialism. It was these people who perpetrated the well-known atrocities of history; but, all things considered, these were untypical aberrations from a widespread Christian sense of right and wrong.

The 20th century saw an aggressive resurgence of the pre-Christian vision of man. The "new morality" is really the "old morality," a throwback to hedonistic materialism. People are treated with callous disregard for human rights and human life. Our century has been stained with ashes and blood—barbed wire, concentration camps, slavery, genocide, mass murder, wars of unprecedented violence, millions of unborn children slain for money. As Pope John Paul II has said: When man repudiates God, he kills himself.

The Old Testament recounts again and again how so many of God's chosen people strayed from the Law of God and adopted the "new morality" of their materialistic neighbors. There's nothing new in what we see around us. Your own generation faces this same choice.

It is our conviction that God will reward or punish each of us for the way we have lived. We adhere to our Christian moral convictions not because of "fashion" but because of our love for God, and for you. We are convinced that your earthly and eternal happiness will depend on your own adoption of our principles. Our Faith has been a patrimony for centuries, since the time when our ancestors were first baptized. You owe it to God and to your children that you internalize these moral principles and pass them on intact to yet another generation. Fashions may come and go, and you may do with these what you wish. But you will answer to God for what you do with your faith, and with that of your children.

Q. *Why do you keep clamping down on me so much? Don't you know that rebelliousness is natural in people my age?*

A. We look forward to the day (coming soon, we trust) when you will have the powers of judgment, responsibility, and self-control in order to direct your own life. Until that time, we're obligated in conscience to give you clear direction from time to time. We do this because we love you and we answer to God for your welfare.

We don't clamp down so much as we channel your powers. Be fair about it. We're not prohibiting anything unreasonably. Sometimes negative guidelines are very helpful in life, even necessary. When you study the "rules of the road" to get your driver's license, you come across dozens of them. They're all reasonable measures to direct your powers of movement; their intent is your own protection and that of others. That's our intent also.

As for rebelliousness, let's look at the issue broadly.

There's nothing wrong with stubbornness—if you're stubborn about the right things. Stubbornness for a good purpose is part of the virtue of fortitude. Even anger is justifiable in the face of outrageous injustice, if your purpose is to correct it. These states of mind are good when they serve the welfare of others. They are wrong when they are self-centered exercises of pride.

Similarly, there's nothing wrong with rebellion—if you are rejecting something reprehensible.

It is normal for people your age to want to be independent. And in fact we want you to be independent: free from childlike needs; independent from negative peer pressure; independent from techniques of mass manipulation and mindless conformity; independent from the allurements of materialism; independent from temptations to abandon your faith.

As we've said, we want you to be really free as soon as possible—a competent, responsible, discriminating adult who freely lives by Christian principles. Regardless of your temporary economic ties to the family, you can become this kind of free person before you're out of your teens. We earnestly hope you do.

You are inclined to rebel? Good, because there's plenty to rebel against. Turn your energetic idealism against evil—pornography, abortion, economic exploitation, political hatred, neglect of the elderly and the poor, and materialism in all its forms.

Save your rebelliousness for those forces in life that threaten your soul, your happiness, and the welfare of your future family. Don't turn it on us, your parents, or the other people who have dedicated themselves to your happiness. This isn't right. It isn't fair.

The Christian ideal implies a vigorous, lifelong rebellion against the notion that man is just a beast. The Church and our society need young people who valiantly maintain this kind of rebellion. Don't ever lose it.

Q. *Why should I bother going to Mass? It's boring, and I get nothing out of it.*

A. The Mass may seem "boring" because of the attitude you bring to it. You have some expectations that are unfulfilled, while you are overlooking a critically important reality. Anyone would be bored under these circumstances.

It's important to understand something clearly: The Mass is not a form of entertainment. Its central purpose is not amusement or pleasant social activity, a shared enjoyment. If you're expecting this, you will probably be disappointed. Who wouldn't be? You see much better quality productions on TV all week; by comparison, what happens in church would strike you as tiresome and repetitive—if, that is, you're looking for entertainment.

But we don't approach the Mass for the feelings it arouses in us. If warm sentiments are aroused, that's fine but it's also beside the point. We attend Mass to give worship to God, and thereby give greater service to other people. It's what we bring to the Mass that counts, not what we take away.

The Mass is a prayer and a sacrifice. It's purpose is to give fitting sacrificial offering to God, to thank him for what he has given to us. This sacrifice is the only perfectly acceptable one because it is made, for all eternity, by the God-man Jesus Christ. During the Mass, we join with Christ, who comes among us through the ministry of the priest, to offer God our honor, praise, sorrow for our sins, and our deepest thanks. This is what we bring. This is why we're there.

Since man is a social being, it's fitting that we should worship together with others. We receive our faith through others. We receive most good things in life from others. Christ himself wanted each of us to be deeply concerned about others; this message runs all through his teachings. Though each of us will die alone, and face judgment alone, we live our faith best on earth in the company and service of others. Each Mass is for the whole Church and for that portion of it present at the Eucharistic sacrifice. We are all bound together—in communion and in Holy Communion— by taking part in the Mass.

All of this means that the Mass is directed to God and to the service of others. It is not directed to superficial feelings.

If you fostered awareness of the great truths in life—who you are, who God is, how much thanks and atonement you owe him—you would find the Mass to be the source and center of your spiritual life. An earnest attitude of prayer and thanksgiving at Mass would bring you, as God's gift in return, a host of spiritual riches: consolation, inner strength, confidence, peace, and a deep happiness that no misfortune could shake. These are incomparably richer than feelings grounded in amusement.

Our Christian forebears approached the Mass this way for centuries. For them, the Eucharistic sacrifice was vitally important. The world's great cathedrals were built literally around the Mass. To take part in the Mass, some of our ancestors risked poverty, imprisonment, social ostracism, and active persecution. This is the exact same Mass that we take part in on Sunday, and throughout the week when we can. God asked our forebears to endure these hardships for the Mass. Perhaps in our own prosperous times, he asks our generation to put up with a little occasional tedium. Maybe, in some ways, our challenge is greater.

The way things are going in our world, your own children will need the graces and strength of our Catholic worship. If you fail to pass it on to them through your own indifference, you will do the gravest injustice to them and to God. You have the power to snuff out, in one generation, the faith that has sustained our family's lineage for centuries. This is an enormous responsibility and you will answer to God for it.

So be patient. Bring an attitude of prayer and thanksgiving to the Mass, and you will find spiritual strength for the challenges that lie awaiting you in life. The riches of God's mercy will give you hope, the Christian symbol of which is the anchor. The Mass will hold you firm and fixed in confidence, while others are battered and set adrift. Let your love for God's sacrifice be a hopeful example to those around you, starting with your own children.

Q. *If I honestly feel that something is right, why can't I go ahead and do it? Shouldn't everyone follow his conscience?*

A. Feelings and conscience are not the same thing.

The conscience is a set of cool-headed, objective, rational criteria—a power of discerning intellect that helps us judge right from wrong. It is the basis for judging the morally right thing to do and the morally wrong thing to avoid; it's a set of standards that we rely upon to assess our responsibilities in different situations.

Like any other serious set of standards, the conscience is formed by study, learning, experience, and instruction. At the most basic level, it starts with an elementary grasp of what is fair (i.e., just) in one's relations with God and with others. This understanding is, throughout life, continually developed and refined by what we learn from others—parents, the Church, others in society whose moral judgment we respect.

We must emphasize that there is a real, objective basis for right and wrong, something wholly apart from our feelings. Regardless of how some people may distort it, ignore it, or deny it, this basis is nonetheless real. It is fundamentally rooted in the nature of man and the nature of God, and the relationship between man and God.

In our own time, the formation of conscience has been distorted by an unrealistic—materialistic—concept of man. Materialism doesn't just mean an attraction to things: to money, to expensive cars and clothes and gadgets. It really means the concept that man is merely a thing. This conception of man has led to several corollary notions, accepted implicitly by so many people around us—that life ends with death; that "God" is just an idea; that moral values are man-made social conventions; that we are not ultimately answerable for the way we live, except to the law; that other people may be treated like things, as in pornography, sexual promiscuity, violence, commercial and political exploitation.

This viewpoint of man and rejection of God was, for a couple of centuries before our era, a kind of intellectual game among philosophers and social thinkers. In the 20th century, we saw its consequences as a program of action. Our own time has seen breathtaking breakthroughs in man's power over nature: air travel, new medicines, plastics, electronics, nuclear energy. Never before has man so successfully controlled and exploited material things.

But, with man seen also as a thing, these same organizational and manipulative powers have wrought horrendous evils as well: concentration camps, genocide, man-made famines, abortion, destruction of whole cities and nations.

If conscience has no basis other than feelings, if there is no objective basis for right and wrong, then how can we condemn the perpetration of these atrocities? A frighteningly large number of the people who carried out these things had no "guilt feelings" whatever. In many cases, they honestly "felt" they were doing some good, or were indifferent to thoughts of right and wrong. The drive for power and the gratification of passions and appetites evoke powerful feelings, and these can smother the voice of conscience.

But we're not just speaking about broad social phenomena here. We're talking about you and the relationship between your conscience and the urges of your lower self.

A large part of your upbringing since infancy has concentrated on your overcoming your feelings. We have tried, through disciplining you, to build your strengths of judgment and will, strengths that are absolutely essential to your earthly happiness and eternal salvation. It's a fact of life that to do the right thing, to live responsibly and morally, to use our powers to give strength to others—these nearly always require us to surpass ourselves, to put our feelings in second place to our duty.

This subordination of feelings is what characterizes responsible adulthood. Though we feel tired, we get up to work in the morning. We keep at work though we feel like quitting. We go without things that please us so that we can provide for our family's needs. We control our passions and appetites in order to live like civilized people and children of God.

There are people your age who have not had a sound formation in conscience. They've had a life-long experience in following their feelings, letting their emotions and wishes be a guide toward action. When these youngsters reach adolescence, they find it very hard to resist the allurements of powerful new sensations—alcohol, drugs, sex, the thrills of vandalism and unrestrained self-indulgence. Pleasures pull them from one thing to another. Many—very many—wind up broken and lonely, sensing at the center of their souls that something is desperately missing.

It's their conscience.

Q. *Adults drink alcohol, which is a drug, but they disapprove of young people using alcohol and other drugs. Isn't this a hypocritical double standard?*

A. One of the signs of intellectual maturity is the ability to make distinctions. Let's make some here.

It's important to realize that the vast majority of adults who drink alcoholic beverages on social occasions do not consume the alcohol primarily as a drug—that is, as a chemical with a psychoactive effect. The alcohol is merely a component of some pleasant-tasting drink, such as wine, beer, or a cocktail. The alcohol is to the beverage as refined sugar is to pastry or ice cream. In other words, normal people ordinarily drink for the overall taste of the beverage, not for its effect on the mind.

Over the centuries, people have found that these beverages, when consumed moderately, add to the enjoyment of meals and other social occasions. These drinks serve a positive good in helping adults to relax and enjoy each other's company (as we know Our Lord and his apostles did). What brings the overall enjoyment here is the conversation, the wit, and the delight of being at ease with friends. The drinks as such are incidental to this pleasure and could even be dispensed with. In fact, if someone were to overindulge in these circumstances, he would be spoiling the occasion for everyone else. (Fact: About one-third of all adults in the United States never drink alcohol at all.)

To get to the point at issue here: The use of recreational drugs differs substantially from the moderate social use of alcoholic beverages. First, drugs are taken in pure form, not for their taste but directly for their psychoactive effect. Secondly, they are not an incidental component of social gatherings. Most users take them alone. When people do gather to take drugs, their principal intent is the drug-taking itself, not the enjoyment of each others' company. The group activity is not so much a social occasion as it is a joint conspiracy of self-centered individuals.

It's critically important not to confuse the legitimate social use of alcohol with the abuse of it. A minority of people do use alcohol directly as a drug. They consume it in any form primarily for its effect on the mind. Their intent is entirely different from that of the rest of the population. These people frequently drink alcohol alone, or they drink immoderately with other alcohol addicts; in this respect, these individuals resemble pure drug users.

Such people are clearly recognized by society as doing harm to themselves and others. If they are addicted to the substance, they are, by definition, problem-drinkers or alcoholics. They're in serious trouble. What they need most is compassionate understanding and professional help.

Here's the key point: All use of recreational drugs is like the abuse of alcohol. Drugs as such, because they are consumed purely for effect, do not have a legitimate social function. Popping pills or smoking dope is not like drinking beer; it is like drinking a lot of beer for the sake of getting drunk, and this is what's wrong.

Of course, aside from the question of clouding the mind, there is another serious moral danger inherent in any drug use. Some people are born with a genetic predisposition to addiction; they can more-or-less easily become hooked to any psychoactive substance. Normally it takes several years for alcohol abuse to become a full-blown alcoholic addiction. But other drugs can cause serious addiction in much less time—in months, weeks, even days. Medical research has established this conclusively. It's another area in which drug use differs significantly from imbibing alcohol.

Literally speaking, a person's lifelong happiness can depend on the avoidance of immoderate alcohol intake and all drug intake. Too many young people have had disastrous experiences with addiction.

Moderate social use of alcohol obviously calls upon sound judgment, some experience with life, and self-control. These things usually grow in strength as you approach adulthood. For this reason, we want you to wait until you are older before you use alcohol outside our supervision. And we earnestly urge you never to try other substances.

It's encouraging to see how so many young people are increasingly staying away from strong alcoholic drinks and overindulgence on social occasions. The tragic deaths of so many people in alcohol-related accidents drives home a message: Alcohol is never to be trifled with, especially by adolescents.

We would hope you will help your friends to see this. Show them, by your example, that you can enjoy life without indulging in drugs of any type. We are confident that you will have the strength of character to do this.

Afterword:
Parent Peer-Support Groups

As you can see by now, this study has dealt mostly with strategic direction, not tactical detail. Each of the issues in these pages could lead to dozens of further questions. What we've tried to do is provide a thought-provoking framework for asking such questions more sharply. How, and under what circumstances, should you take specific action with your teens later on? And how can you best articulate your principles to them?

You can find helpful answers to these and other questions by discussing adolescent issues with other parents, especially "veterans." Discussions with other couples are extremely helpful, and they're richly rewarding as well, sometimes in unexpected ways.

Our society has many support groups which do enormous good for their participants. Alcoholics Anonymous has helped countless families. So has the Tough-Love organization for parents of uncontrollable children. Associations of adoptive parents, local parent-teacher groups, societies for parents of drug-addictive children—all have done great good for their participants. It's as if our society has rediscovered the value and necessity of having close, supportive friends.

Acquaintances are different from friends. Dealing with acquaintances never seems to get beyond small talk. In superficial social settings, you talk about local politics, local sports, issues in the news, even the weather, but not much more. With friends, on the other hand, you can talk about anything. You can talk about the matters closest to your private self—your personal history, your personal mistakes and successes, your concerns for the future, your hopes and concerns for your children.

Our point is this: When couples meet to discuss their children's upbringing, they usually become warm friends, often lifelong friends. When people open their minds and hearts to each other, they seem to form a strong spiritual bond that lasts for years. Shared values and mutually pledged support serve to bond people together more strongly than anything outside family love. (Alcoholics Anonymous has experienced this for years; members typically become friends for life.)

So, we would urge you to find other couples and befriend them this way. You need each other now and you can rely on each other later, when the children are growing through adolescence.

There are any number of ways to go about this sort of parent-to-parent discussion. Let me outline here some approaches that other parents have found effective:

1. Keep it simple. The simpler, the better. Most parents today are much too busy to go in for large-group lectures or complicated lesson-plans. Meeting in your home with two to four couples is much more manageable.

2. Give a copy of this book to other couples you know, perhaps parents whose children are in school with your own. Ask them to read it and see if they're interested in meeting from time to time to talk about the issues outlined herein. You may be surprised to find out how many other parents share your concern for the children's future lives as adolescents. Agree to meet for a planning session.

3. When you meet, write out a list of topics that everyone agrees upon. You might want to follow the

sequence of Q/A's listed here, or go first through the description of typical adolescent characteristics. For that matter, you might want to discuss material from other books on the subject. It doesn't matter what agenda you pick, as long as it's an agreed-upon list.

4. People have found that a biweekly or monthly meeting works best, usually on a weeknight or Sunday afternoon. Kids can come along if they can play somewhere else in the house, fairly close nearby. (By the way, it's excellent for children to see their parents enjoy themselves with close friends. In our society, this is an infrequent occurrence.)

5. Choose one topic for discussion, with a backup from the next issue on the list. If you go through the main topic to everyone's satisfaction and you have time, you can start on the backup.

6. How to prepare for discussion? The best way is to search your memory. Everybody has been through adolescence, and everyone had friends at the time. Search for personal examples from your own history, what you went through, how you think things are different today, how you wish you could do things differently, and the like. Draw examples and observations from what you know about in your own community, too. (But be careful to observe anonymity; don't mention people's names.) In other words, the discussion should be anecdotal, not theoretical. Conversation like this is lively and often humorous. Avoid over-earnestness. A serious subject need not be treated heavy-handedly. Strive in this, as in so much of family life, to be serious of purpose but light in touch. This does wonders for your confidence.

7. At some point, maybe from the beginning, invite older, more experienced couples to your meetings. They have a lot to say that's helpful. If they have sufficient notice to think about the topic, they

should come up with a great many personal experiences. One approach is for them to consider this question: "If we had to do it all over again, this is what we'd do...." And then they can explain why.

8. Some groups have found it useful to keep a written account of ideas that surface in each meeting with each couple getting a photocopy to keep. Some even make an audio-tape of the meeting to lend to couples who were unable to attend. (Occasional absences are inevitable.)

9. Finally, members of the group should do other activities together. Invariably, once friendship is formed, they find that they want to. Couples could join each other for picnics, ball games, watching sports events on TV, and the like. One of the very best activities is an annual spiritual retreat. The more you explore the issues of adolescence, the more you realize the importance of prayer.

These are the essential points. As you can see, forming a support group like this is really quite simple and even enjoyable. Most of all, it's invaluable. Why not give it a try with some of your friends? You and your children, now and later, have a lot to gain.

Personal Notes